How to Rest in Your Season of Singleness

20 Day Devotional

ARIEL GREEN

How to Rest in Your Season of Singleness: 20 Day Devotional
Copyright ©2021 by Ariel Green
ISBN: 9781737708759

Unless otherwise indicated, all scripture quotations are taken from the New Living Translation, Copyright (c) 1996, 2004, 2015, by Tyndale House Foundation. Used by permission of Tyndale House Publishers Inc., Carol Stream, Illinois 60188. All rights reserved.

Scripture quotations marked (KJV) are taken from the Holy bible, King James Version (Public Domain)

Scripture quotations marked (KJV) are from The Authorized (King James) Version. Rights in the Authorized Version in the United Kingdom are vested in the Crown. Reproduced by permission of the Crown's patentee, Cambridge University Press

All rights reserved. No part of this publication may be reproduced, stored in a retrieval system, or transmitted in any form or by any means, electronic, mechanical, photocopying or otherwise, without the prior permission of the copyright owner.

ALL RIGHTS RESERVED

Printed in the U.S.A.

To the singles who are struggling in their season of singleness and looking for something or someone to hold. I was once in your shoes, trying to find peace in the season. Hang in there — God is with you. Cling to Him. May He forever be your solid rock throughout your journey in life.

Contents

Day 1· Be Still	9
Day 2· Rest in God	11
Day 3· Devote Yourself to God	13
Day 4· Receive Peace	15
Day 5· Worship God	19
Day 6· Be Content	21
Day 7· Heal and Become Whole	25
Day 8· Me, Myself, & God	29
Day 9· Date God	33
Day 10· Boundaries	37
Day 11· Seek God Above all Else	41
Day 12· Focus	45
Day 13· Temptation	49
Day 14· Rest in God's Love	53
Day 15· Rest in God's Presence	55
Day 16· Righteousness and Purity	57
Day 17· Purpose of Singleness	61
Day 18· Pray for Godly Friends	63
Day 19· Wait on God	65
Day 20· Forever Single	69

- Day 1 -
Be Still

"Be still in the presence of the Lord and wait
patiently for him to act..."
Psalms 37:7 NLT

Rest means to be still. To rest, it means to be still in your mind, in your pursuit, and in your will. Many times, it can be challenging for us to rest and momentarily cease striving in life due to us wanting to be in control of our destiny. In order to learn how to rest in your season of singleness, you must first learn how to rest in God.

Resting in God means to trust in Him. You must believe that He knows what's best for you in life. When you truly trust someone in a relationship, you believe they have your best interest in mind. You can rely on them in time of need. You do not worry because you know they are going to come through for you, and you are confident in them. This is how God desires for you to rest in your relationship with Him. Resting in God is not always easy because we do not always see the work, He is doing around us or behind the scenes. You must trust that He has everything under control in your singleness and future. God is taking care of you. Be confident in Him!

Trusting in God requires faith. Hebrews 11:3 says, it is "By faith we understand the entire universe was formed at God's command that for what we now see did not come from anything than can be seen. "It was by faith we believe God created it. So, by faith, you must believe God is protecting, holding, and keeping you safe in this season. He has everything under control. Your future is in His hands. You are right where you need to be. Trust Him, rest, and be still!

> "Be still and know that I am God! I will be honored by every nation. I will be honored throughout the world. The Lord of Heaven's Armies is here among us [you]; the God of Israel is our [your] fortress [defender]."
> Psalms 46:10-11 NLT

- Day 2 -
Rest in God

"This is what the Sovereign Lord, the Holy One of Israel, says· "Only in returning to me and resting in me will you be saved. In quietness and confidence is your strength."
Isaiah 30·15 NLT

As you go through this day, remember to rest in God. Find a quiet place as you start or end your day to rest in God's love and bask in His presence. Sit still for a minute and allow the Holy Spirit to speak to your heart. Turn off the television, radio, or any other electronic device to which you are tempted to give your attention. Sit in silence. Meditate on a scripture and apply it to your life. Think about the cross and how much Christ, the Son of God, loves you. His love for you is still great. Nothing in life will ever separate you from God's love which is revealed through the death of Jesus Christ, your Lord and Savior. No fear, shame, failure, sin, guilt, heartache, or mistake can separate you from the love of Jesus. Rest in God's love today.

"Can anything ever separate us from Christ's love? Does it mean he no longer loves us if we have trouble, calamity, or are persecuted, or hungry, or destitute, or in danger, or threatened with death? (As the Scripture say, "For your sake we are killed every day, we are being slaughtered like sheep.") No, despite all these things, overwhelming victory is ours through Christ, who loved us. And I am convinced that nothing can ever separate us from God's love. Neither death nor life, neither angels nor demons, neither our fears for today or worries about tomorrow-not even the powers of hell can separate us from God's love. No power in the sky above or in the earth below-indeed, nothing in all creation will ever be able to separate us from the love of God that is revealed in Christ Jesus our Lord."
Romans 8:35-39 NLT

- Day 3 -
Devote Yourself to God

"Therefore, my beloved brethren, be ye steadfast, unmovable, always abounding, in the work of the Lord, for as much as ye know that your labor is not in vain in the Lord."
1 Corinthians 15:58 KJV

Devote yourself to God today. Do not go through this day asking God to do this or take care of that. Take a break for one minute, stop worshiping your prayers, and put your attention on God's presence. When you truly devote yourself to the Lord, you give up more of your time and focus on ways to become more intimate in your relationship with Him. Read your Bible, and take notes on what you read, deeply study God's word. Work on building a solid and unbreakable bond with God. Ask God to help you better understand Him, His word, and His ways. Secure a stronger foundation in Him. No matter what comes or goes, who leaves or stays in your life, your devotion to God should be unwavering. Abide in Him.

HOW TO REST IN YOUR SEASON OF SINGLENESS

"Anyone who listens to my teaching and follows it is wise, like a person who builds a house on a solid rock. Though the rain comes in torrents and the flood waters rise and the winds beat against that house, it won't collapse because it was built on bedrock. But anyone who hears my teaching and doesn't obey it is foolish, like a person who builds a house on sand. When the rain and floods come and the winds beat against that house, it will collapse with a mighty crash."
Matthew 7:24-27 NLT

- Day 4 -
Receive Peace

Peace is a promise God keeps. Isaiah 26:3 says, "You will keep in perfect peace all who trust in you, all whose thoughts are fixed on you." Keeping your mind fixed on God can sometimes be a struggle, especially if your mind is cluttered with stress, worries, and problems. The first step in regaining control of your mind during a crazy moment is to whisper these words a few times. "Peace, be still." Thoughts in your head will soon begin to unravel and settle into a place of peace as you command them to go. If you strive to discover the beauty of God in everything—in your day, in the sky, in your struggles, and in the simple things, He will lead your mind into peace. Practice fixing your mind on God, something peaceful, and on something positive as you go through your day. Do not complain. Remember peace is a promise God keeps. It is always near to you. You must work and choose to protect the peace the Lord has given you. Do not let anything rob you of your peace.

Affirmation

I command peace on my job. I command peace in my home. I command peace in my family. I command peace in my heart. I command peace in my mind. I command peace in my relationships. I command peace in my friendships. I command peace in my singleness. I command peace today.

"I am leaving you with a gift - peace of mind and heart. And the peace I give is a gift the world cannot give. So don't be troubled or afraid."
John 15:27 NLT

Prayer

Dear Lord,

Renew my mind and help me walk in peace. Give me peace in the midst of difficulties, chaos, and hardships. Bring peace out of the current pain and confusion I am experiencing. Teach me how to guard my thoughts and protect the peace you have given me. Help me to continue to fix my mind on you in my season of singleness. Calm the storm within me. Father, be my peace. I need you! Amen.

HOW TO REST IN YOUR SEASON OF SINGLENESS

- Day 5 -
Worship God

> "Worship the Lord with gladness. Come before him, singing with joy. Acknowledge that the Lord is God! He made us, and we are his. We are his people, the sheep of his pasture."
> Psalms 100·2-3 NLT

In your free time today, take a moment to admire and worship God. To worship means to express or show reverence. Worship God in your own creative way such as singing, writing, dancing, or speaking to tell God how you feel. Worship God for who He is, what He's done, and what He will do! Continue to believe God for good things. Believe things will get better for you in this season. God is good in every moment in your life, especially singleness. There is so much purpose in it. God wants your attention and to solely pursue you before a man pursues you. As you worship and trust God more in this season, He will reveal things to you about the vision you have concerning the man of God for whom you've been praying. Thank God, and worship Him in this season.

> "For everything there is a season, a time for every activity under heaven. A time to be born and a time to die. A time to plant and a time to harvest. A time to kill and a time to heal. A time to tear down and a time to build up. A time to cry and a time to laugh. A time to grieve and a time to dance. A time to scatter stones and a time to gather stones. A time to embrace and a time to turn away. A time to search and a time to quit searching. A time to keep and a time to throw away. A time to tear and a time to mend. A time to be quiet and a time to speak. A time to love and a time to hate. A time for war and a time for peace. What do people really get for all their hard work? I have seen the burden God has placed on us all. Yet God has made everything beautiful for its own time..."
> Ecclesiastes 3: 1-11 NLT

- Day 6 -
Be Content

Be content with where you are in life because being single is only for a season. When you first enter this world, you are a newborn baby. In another season, you grow to be a toddler, school-aged, and then adolescent. Before you realize it, you will be married. The season you are currently in is only temporary. It will pass in God's time, so do not rush out of it; enjoy it!

Contentment is a state of mind. To be content means to be satisfied with what you have or where you are in life. The Bible talks about how true godliness with contentment is itself great wealth (1 Timothy 6:6). Paul, an Apostle of God, wrote half the New Testament. He was a messenger from God who laid the foundation for the Church and taught other Christians how to live a righteous life unto God. During his imprisonment for Christ, Paul wrote a letter to the people in Philippi. In this letter, he discussed how he learned to be content with what he had during his suffering for Christ. Paul says, "I know how to live on almost nothing or with everything. I have learned the secret of living in every situation, whether it is with a full stomach or empty, with plenty or little. For I can do everything through Christ who gives me strength (Philippians 4:12-13)." Here, while in prison, Paul is encouraging people in Philippi to be content and continue to endure through their hardships and persecutions with God.

No matter what you lack, whether it's food, security, comfort, love, happiness, friends, you name it, you must learn how to be content with your relationship with Christ. Christ must be enough for you because only Christ can fulfill your deepest and most internal needs. Whatever you lack, Jesus is full of. He will fulfill all of your needs (situational, emotional, and financial). Keep pressing on! In due time, things will get better and work in your favor. Become more satisfied with the Lord in this moment and in every other season after this. Your life is worth more than fulfilling a relationship status. Be content and complete your season of singleness.

"After all, we brought nothing with us when we came into the world, and we can't take anything with us when we leave it. So, if we have enough food and clothing, let us be content."
1 Timothy 6:7 NLT

5 things I can do to become more content in my singleness.
(Ideas: Express gratitude, be creative, draw, spend less time on social media, enjoy family, enjoy nature, serve others, read, etc.)

1. _____
_____
_____

2. _____
_____
_____

3. _____
_____
_____

4. _____
_____
_____

5. _____
_____
_____

- Day 7 -
Heal and Become Whole

Healing is necessary in this season. Before you bring another person into your life, you must be released from past bondage. We all have some pain, adversity, or childhood/adulthood trauma that transpired in our life we must heal from. Maybe, you have a relationship with a family member, friend, or ex that is toxic to you from which you need to be delivered. Maybe, you need to grieve a recent death and bring your hurt and distress about this matter to our Lord. The more issues you have individually, the more challenging it will be to soar, fight, and thrive in a marriage or relationship with someone else. Singleness is the perfect time to work on you! Think of it as a time to prepare for your future spouse and become the woman of God you need to be without strings attached to anyone else. Talk about Freedom! Work on becoming the best version of yourself. Conquer your mental health issues with God and become more secure in yourself. Ask and allow the

Holy Spirit to lead you to other resources to help get to the root of your personal problems.

During the moments you experience discomfort or loneliness in this season, God can fill the void(s) in your life. God will fill that empty space with his love, truth, and Spirit if you let Him. He will comfort you in your separation. Healing is necessary for several areas· your mind, body, soul, and spirit. Confront and get to the bottom of your issues. When you do, very soon, you will begin to walk in everlasting joy and freedom!

> "So, you also are complete through your
> union with Christ, who is the head over
> every ruler and authority."
> Colossians 2· 10 NLT

3 things I need healing or deliverance from:

1. _____

_____

_____

2. _____

_____

_____

3. _____

_____

_____

HOW TO REST IN YOUR SEASON OF SINGLENESS

- Day 8 -
Me, Myself, & God - I Love You

As you continue to work through your issues, do not be afraid to spend quality time with yourself. Most women are uncomfortable spending time alone with themselves for many reasons. Some women do not like being alone. Other ladies would rather be in the presence of a man or others and enjoy their company versus their own. But how do you expect someone in a relationship to understand you if you don't fully know yourself and spend time with yourself? Do you even truly know what love is? How much do you really love yourself and God? This is your time to enjoy your own company!

Your fear of being alone in public and by yourself is holding you back from full recovery. Get out of your own way! Really, what shame is there in being alone and doing things alone? Jesus was the most powerful man on earth and did most of His work alone with the help of His disciples. This is your season to be in solitude with God. Peel back the ugly layers of hurt, discomfort, and fear, and start spending more time getting to know YOU with God. Don't be afraid to start saying "no" to others and "yes" to yourself. You will discover many new things about yourself like who you truly are in Christ and what God thinks about you. Your identity will be renewed, confirmed, and strengthened. As a woman, you will become more secure in your self-worth, gifts, skills, and abilities.

> "O Lord, you have examined my heart and know everything about me. You know when I sit down or stand up. You know my thoughts even when I'm far away. You see me when I travel and when I rest at home. You know everything I do. You know what I am going to say even before I say it, Lord. You go before me and follow me. You place your hand of blessing on my head. Such knowledge is too wonderful for me, too great for me to understand! I can never escape from your Spirit! I can never get away from your presence! If I go up to heaven, you are there; if I go down to the grave, you are

there. If I ride the wings of the morning, if I dwell by the farthest oceans, even there your hand will guide me, and your strength will support me. I could ask the darkness to hide me and the light around me to become night—but even in darkness I cannot hide from you. To you the night shines as bright as day. Darkness and light are the same to you. You made all the delicate, inner parts of my body and knit me together in my mother's womb. Thank you for making me so wonderfully complex! Your workmanship is marvelous— how well I know it. You watched me as I was being formed in utter seclusion, as I was woven together in the dark of the womb. You saw me before I was born. Every day of my life was recorded in your book. Every moment was laid out before a single day had passed. How precious are your thought about me, O God! They cannot be numbered! I can't even count them; they outnumber the grains of sand! And when I wake up, you are still with me!"

Psalm 139·1-18 NLT

HOW TO REST IN YOUR SEASON OF SINGLENESS

5 things about myself I need to love and embrace more:

1. _____
_____
_____

2. _____
_____
_____

3. _____
_____
_____

4. _____
_____
_____

5. _____
_____
_____

- Day 9 -

Date God

> "Come close to God, and God will come close to you. Wash your hands, you sinners; purify your hearts, for your loyalty is divided between God and the world."
> James 4:8 NLT

As you continue to spend time with yourself, invite God into your day. Include Him in your agenda today and your weekend plans. Your relationship with God is the most important relationship in your life. If you do not nurture it, it will die. If you do not spend time with God, you will miss out on instruction from Him. Relationships are a two-way street—you must meet the other person halfway. A relationship is a give and take, it requires teamwork, intentionality, and effort. It takes two willing partners to make it work. Your relationship with God is the same way.

Talk to God like He is your friend. Be real with yourself and Him. Do not be afraid to be vulnerable and intimate with God about your thoughts and emotions. God already knows everything about you because He created you. He formed you in your mother's womb. Yes, He is invisible, but His presence is always around and near to you. God wants to be closer to you but will not force Himself on you because He is a gentleman. He respects your free will. God is always knocking on the door of our hearts, but it is up to us whether or not we will let Him in.

In your alone time, be more intentional with inviting God into your day. Have fun with Him. Sit in the park with God. Go on ice cream dates with God. Do all things with Him. Make this a routine, and He will begin to solidify more truths in you about yourself and future. Give your love to Him and receive His love for you. As you date God, you will learn what you should and should not expect from a man in a relationship. Your expectations will develop while you're single and become clearer to you. You will discover how you desire to be treated and respected by men. You will also learn how to communicate your boundaries and expectations. God will show you His standard of love.

"Take delight [pleasure/satisfaction] in the Lord, and he will give you your heart's desires."
Proverbs 37:4 NLT

Prayer

Dear Lord,

Fill me with Your love. Fill my heart, brokenness, and emptiness with Your love. When it feels like no one is near, comfort me Father, because I desperately need Your love. Give me the love that I have never experienced. I need the love that I have been missing. Surround me with Your loving presence. I want to experience Your love today. Amen.

- Day 10 -
Boundaries

Boundaries are guidelines and rules to protect you from hurt or danger. Boundaries are important in relationships because they help keep us safe. In the book of Genesis, God created the Heavens and the Earth. God planted a garden in Eden and instructed Adam and Eve which trees from which they could and could not eat. God told Adam and Eve in Genesis 2:16, "You may freely eat the fruit of every tree in the garden- except the tree of the knowledge of good and evil. If you eat its fruit, you are sure to die." Later in the chapter, the serpent deceived the woman, and she ate a fruit from the tree and gave some to her husband. Immediately after this act, the Lord God reminded Adam and Eve they would die and stated the consequences they would face in their future due to their disobedience.

In this story, we see how God established firm and clear boundaries with Adam and Eve. He communicated these boundaries to them ahead of time. He wanted to protect them from many things, not just the knowledge of good and evil, but from overall confusion, deceptions, and destruction in life. Boundaries are vital! You must begin to establish boundaries in singleness to prevent you from falling. Establish boundaries in your relationships, on your job, places you go, activities you partake in, and in any other area(s) of your life. At first, boundaries may be difficult to maintain, but if you keep communicating and practicing them, they will become easier to maintain. Do not be afraid to set boundaries with family members, friends, or male individuals. Remember, boundaries are for your protection. They will help keep you close to God, away from sin, and out of trouble and heartache. Ask the Holy Spirit to show you what areas in your life you need to create better boundaries in and do it!

> "Guard your heart above all else, for it determines the course of your life."
> Proverbs 4:23 NLT

What areas in my life do I need to enforce clear boundaries?

1. _____

_____

_____

2. _____

_____

_____

3. _____

_____

_____

4. _____

_____

_____

5. _____

_____

_____

HOW TO REST IN YOUR SEASON OF SINGLENESS

- Day 11 -
Seek God Above All Else

Seek God today. The Bible says it plain and clear in Matthew 6:31-34, "So, don't worry about these things, saying what will we eat? What will we drink? What will we wear? These things dominate the mind [thoughts] of unbelievers [those who have no faith/trust in God's word/power; carnal] but your heavenly Father already knows all of your needs. Seek the Kingdom of God above all else and live righteously and he will give you everything you need. So don't worry about tomorrow, for tomorrow will bring its own worries. Today's trouble is enough for today."

You must learn to seek God's face, not his hand. Seek His presence, His glory, His ways, His peace, His love, His heart, His truths, HIM—do not seek things! It is important to seek God wholeheartedly without ceasing. To seek means to pursue. It means to long for, run, or strive after. Instead of striving after things and the blessings of God, God's Word instructs to seek Him

FIRST, then these things will come. Everything else will be added.

> *When you are feeling lonely, seek God not man or people.*
>
> *When you have no friends, seek God's friendship.*
>
> *Instead of chasing money, seek God, He will provide a way out of no way.*
>
> *Instead of trying to maintain or chase someone in a relationship, seek God's relationship. Learn to be content with Him.*
>
> *Instead of seeking after cars, clothes, or material things, seek God, He will give you an identity and glow so greater than these things.*
>
> *Instead of chasing a job you don't have yet, seek God. He will reveal your purpose to you.*

When you are seeking God, it is important not to worry about your future. Faith and fear cannot live together. They do not mix. You must choose one or the other. Your anxieties and worries will get you nowhere. Instead, it will slow you down mentally, physically, spiritually, and emotionally. It will weigh you down and hinder your progress and growth. God knows you want to know the outcome of your situation, but He also wants you to trust in Him and seek Him above your worries and plans. He knows what is best for you in this season and what you need in the future. God said in His word that He will give you everything you need, so do not worry about tomorrow (Matthew 6:33). His word says, "I will withhold no good thing from those who do what is right" (Psalm 84:11). Give Him your faith and be still! Remember, He is God and in control. Trust Him, rest, and believe! When the time is right, He will make it all happen.

> "That is why I tell you not to worry about everyday life—whether you have enough food and drink, or enough clothes to wear. Isn't life more than food, and your body

more than clothing? Look at the birds. They don't plant or harvest or store food in barns, for your heavenly Father feeds them. And aren't you far more valuable to him than they are? Can all your worries add a single moment to your life? And why worry about your clothing? Look at the lilies of the field and how they grow. They don't work or make their clothing, yet Solomon in all his glory was not dressed as beautifully as they are. And if God cares so wonderfully for wildflowers that are here today and thrown into the fire tomorrow, he will certainly care for you. Why do you have so little faith?"
Matthew 6:25-30 NLT

- Day 12 -

Focus

"Set your mind and keep focused habitually on the things above [the heavenly things], not on things that are on the earth [which have only temporal value]. For you died [to this world], and your [new real] life is hidden with Christ in God."
Colossians 3:2-3 AMP

Where is your mind wandering to today? Do you wander or wonder often? When you wonder, you are curious or in awe of something. But to wander means to roam freely without a sense of direction.

Take control of your thoughts and feelings in your singleness. The enemy wants you to have a pity party and to think this will be the worst time of your life. He does not want you to move forward and enjoy being single. The devil wants to use men and other circumstances to distract you and break your focus in this season. He does not want you to pass this test alone with God. Do not let your emotions, positive or negative, get the best of you in this season. Talk to God and tell

Him how you feel; He cares! Release your feelings to Him, then return your attention to Jesus.

You still have work to do, purpose to fulfill, a race to finish, and an assignment to complete on earth! Lift your head up and put your eyes on Jesus. Look around and see how blessed you are. God woke you up this morning; you are breathing. Therefore, do not focus on that relationship or other things you do not have. Focus on what you do have and be grateful. Today you are living, so make it great!

> "Give all your worries and cares to God, for he cares about you. Stay Alert! Watch out for your great enemy, the devil. He prowls around like a roaring lion, looking for someone to devour. Stand firm against him and be strong in your faith. Remember that your family of believers all over the world is going through the same kind of suffering you are. In his kindness God called you to share in his eternal glory by means of Christ Jesus, so after you have suffered a little while, he will restore, support and strengthen you, and he will place you on a firm foundation. All power to him forever! Amen."
> 1 Peter 5:7-11 NLT

- Day 13 -

Temptation

> "God blesses those who patiently endure testing and temptation. Afterward they will receive the crown of life that God has promised to those who love him. And remember, when you are being tempted, do not say, "God is tempting me." God is never tempted to do wrong, and he never tempts anyone else. Temptation comes from our own desires, which entice us and drag us away. These desires give birth to sinful actions. And when sin is allowed to grow, it gives birth to death."
> James 1· 12-15 NLT

In this season, you are going to be tempted in your flesh in many ways, especially to move ahead of God and settle with a guy in a relationship. So, how will you know when it's time to move into a relationship with a potential suitor? Answer· The more you rest in God, the less anxious you will be about the timing. Rest and be still in Him! When it's time to move out of your season of singleness, you will have peace; there will be peace in your relationship. You will not feel pressured, apprehensive, or confused, about moving forward.

Instead, there will be freedom in your decision to date again when you resolve to do it God's way. Remember, first you must become content in your relationship with Christ. Christ must be enough for you. Let him fill your thirst for love and relationship.

The less content you are with being single, the more difficult you will make things for yourself in the present and future. You will prolong your season of singleness. Continue to ask the Holy Spirit to help you endure in this time and be satisfied with Him! Allow God to pursue you. Your soul is longing to be connected to your Creator and Heavenly Father. Only God can fill the void and heal the insecurity within you. He is all your soul needs in this season. Allow Him to dig out, fill, and heal your wound with His perfect love (1 John 4:18).

> "But my God shall supply all your need [physical, social, emotional, parental, financial, any uncommon need] according to his riches in glory by Christ Jesus."
> Philippians 4:19 KJV

A Message from God

Be still and allow Me to prepare you for the promise. You are not fully prepared for what is coming. Walk with Me. Yield your desires and will to Me, in return for mine. In this season, I am the One who you need the most, the Lord your God, the great I Am. Do not abort the process and pain you experience, for it will lead you to the promise. It is necessary. I will be everything you need and more.

HOW TO REST IN YOUR SEASON OF SINGLENESS

- Day 14 -

Rest in God's Love

"I am the way, the truth, and the life. No one can come to the Father except through me."
John 14: 7 NLT

God loves you so much. He sent Jesus Christ to die on the cross for humanity's sins. Sin is anything we partake in that is outside of the character of Jesus. Jesus came to earth and died because people were lost, rebellious, and disobedient towards God's law, the Ten Commandments. The Ten Commandments were a set of guidelines for believers to follow. The world was living in darkness and needed a savior. The Ten Commandments were not enough. So, God sent His only Son, Jesus Christ, to be the example to the world, to give holy direction, and to show others how to truly live a righteous life as a believer and follower of Christ.

Jesus was the ultimate light. He also taught the Word of God to people. Christ was eventually beaten and hung on a cross because many did not want to believe He was the Son of God. He was hated for the love, compassion, integrity, power, and righteous lifestyle He demonstrated. As a result, he was crucified. Christ suffered and died so you could live again and find life in Him. His death was the ultimate sacrifice of love. God loves you so much that He sent His only Son to come to Earth to show you the way to freedom and to guide and lead you to Him. Not only does God love you, but so does Jesus. Jesus loved you enough to obey His father's difficult instructions; He died to prove that His love for you is real. Rest in God's love today.

> "For God so loved the world, that he gave his only begotten Son, that whosoever believeth in him should not perish, but have everlasting life."
> John 3:16 KJV

- Day 15 -
Relax in God's Presence

Today, give your anxious thoughts to the Lord because He did not create you to worry. Ask the Holy Spirit to take control of your thoughts and receive peace again. Allow the presence of God to fill your space. Inhale peace and exhale worry. Inhale confidence and exhale doubt. Inhale faith and exhale fear. Inhale peace and exhale anxiety. What you are worrying about in this season, God has already worked out in another season. Be still, sit in silence, and relax in His presence. Invite God into your space.

> "Don't worry about anything; instead pray about everything. Tell God what you need and thank Him for all he has done. Then you will experience God's peace, which exceeds anything we can understand. His peace will guard your hearts and minds as you live in Christ Jesus."
> Philippians 4:6 NLT

HOW TO REST IN YOUR SEASON OF SINGLENESS

- Day 16 -
Righteousness and Purity

> "All scripture is inspired by God and is useful to teach us what is true and to make us realize what is wrong in our lives. It corrects us when we are wrong and teaches us to do what is right. God uses it to prepare and equip his people to do every good work."
>
> 2 Timothy 3:16-17 NLT

Purity means free from contamination. When something is pure, it is clean. There are many things that can contaminate someone and make a person impure. What you watch, a disturbing experience, what you indulge, your environment, one's lifestyle and so on. Whenever contamination takes place, it affects four areas: the mind, body, soul, and spirit. We all have participated in and been through things in life that were not sanctioned by God and made us impure. No matter what the sin is that made you impure, whether you pursued it, or it was brought upon you, there is freedom, hope, and new life in the name Jesus. Christ is your redeemer!

As you spend more time with God, He will reveal His plan of righteousness to you. God will show you the sin in your life you need to identify and confess and from which you need to repent. He will teach you and show you how to pursue things in life His way. We all have sinned and fallen short of the glory of God, but God gives us grace to get things right. As you rest in your season of singleness, the Holy Spirit will help you. Use this time to get things in order in your life. Make the necessary changes within yourself. Work on your character, your attitude, and daily apply to your life what you learn from the Word of God. At first, it will be a challenge, but do not grow weary of doing God's will. God will honor your obedience and sacrifice towards Him for doing the right thing. As you spend time with Him, God will give you brand new desires for your life. These desires will be pure, holy, and righteous. They will lead you to godly success.

> "Teach me your ways, O Lord, that I may live according to your truth! Grant me purity of heart, so that I may honor you."
> Psalms 86:11 NLT

"Since you have heard about Jesus and have learned the truth that comes from him, throw off your old sinful nature and your former way of life, which is corrupted by lust and deception. Instead, let the Spirit renew your thoughts and attitudes. Put on your new nature, created to be like God—truly righteous and holy. So stop telling lies. Let us tell our neighbors the truth, for we are all parts of the same body. And "don't sin by letting anger control you." Don't let the sun go down while you are still angry, for anger gives a foothold to the devil. If you are a thief, quit stealing. Instead, use your hands for good hard work, and then give generously to others in need. Don't use foul or abusive language. Let everything you say be good and helpful, so that your words will be an encouragement to those who hear them. And do not bring sorrow to God's Holy Spirit by the way you live. Remember, he has identified you as his own, guaranteeing that you will be saved on the day of redemption. Get rid of all bitterness, rage, anger, harsh words, and slander, as well as all types of evil behavior. Instead, be kind to each other, tenderhearted, forgiving one another, just as God through Christ has forgiven you."
Ephesians 4:21-32 NLT

Prayer for Purity

Dear Lord,

Help me maintain a pure lifestyle as I strive to honor You. Increase discipline and self-control within me. Help me to surrender to Your Word, Your voice, and Your spirit, and help me to die to my flesh. When I am weak, I know You are making me strong, so the enemy will not weaken me even more. Renew my mind once again, and empower me to continue my walk-in purity, freedom, and righteousness. I will pass this test, and all of the glory will go to you, in Jesus's name, I pray, Amen.

- Day 17 -
Purpose of Singleness

Many women often feel frustrated, hopeless, and alone in their season of singleness. While these feelings and emotions are normal, some women do not understand what God is doing during this time, why they are single, or why no one is pursuing them. Some ladies think this season is tough and never-ending, others think they are supposed to be in a relationship with a man and find "the one" in this season. Though all these feelings and emotions are normal, the only man you should be in a relationship with is God, the Man above. He is the One you need to be with during this time.

The Bible informs us that a man who finds a wife finds a treasure, and he receives favor from the Lord (Proverbs 18:22). The man God has for you will chase God first, then you. He will find you in the Lord's time! He will pursue you and be intentional with you.

God is a jealous God. He wants you to be closer to Him than any man or person on Earth. He is jealous about

His relationship with you. Be more intimate with God in this season and spend quality time with Him daily! He wants to be closer to you. At times, your singleness will be tough, but God will strengthen you in it and help you endure. His grace is all you need. God's power works best in your weakness (2 Corinthians 12·9). The purpose of your singleness is to discover your purpose in God, become whole while growing into the woman of God you were pre-destined to be. This time is so vital. Be still and allow God to make you more beautiful in this season. You will discover many things with Him.

> "Don't copy the behavior and customs of this world, but let God transform you into a new person by changing the way you think. Then you will learn to know God's will for you, which is good and pleasing and perfect."
> Romans 12·2 NLT

- Day 18 -

Pray for Godly Friends

"As iron sharpens iron, so a friend sharpens a friend."
Proverbs 27:17 NLT

In this season, allow God to be your best friend; become more comfortable confiding in Him. Vent to God. He is always present in your life even when you don't feel Him. God is always listening. You must trust and believe He is always with you. Listen for His voice. God will send the Holy Spirit to be a personal helper for you to reassure and clarify His love and truths to you (John 14:15-17). The Holy Spirit is a messenger from God who speaks in a still, small voice.

Befriend God and ask Him to put people in your life who are like-minded and mature in their walk with Him. Pray for positive and godly leaders with whom you can fellowship and from whom you can learn. Pray for sharper discernment. Ask God to bless you with girlfriends/women who are serious about their walk with Christ and have your best interest at heart. Finally, ask God to show you how to be a friend to the women He puts in your life. As you grow in the Lord, your friendships will change. Stay humble and be teachable because your spiritual eyes will become more open. You will start to recognize which relationships are toxic, stagnant, and pull you away from Christ. Don't be alarmed; instead, let go of whoever God is telling you to leave behind and trust Him. He has a master plan. He knows who is best for you. Do not be afraid to share with others what God is doing in your life. He wants you to be bold, strong, and courageous in your faith. Stay confident in Him. As God removes and brings people in your life, be patient with Him, yourself, and others. He is still working things out in both you and them.

> "Run from anything that stimulates youthful lusts. Instead, pursue righteous living, faithfulness, love, and peace. Enjoy the companionship of those who call on the Lord with pure hearts."
> 2 Timothy 2:22 NLT

- Day 19 -
Wait on God

"But if we look forward to something we don't have yet, we must wait patiently and confidently."
Romans 8:25 NLT

While you continue to rest and be still in God in your singleness, wait on Him! Wait on God to move in your life. He will move you out of your single state. While you are waiting for this time to end, do not hope for a man to come in and sweep you off your feet. Instead, have faith, believe, and put your hope in God. Do not compare the time you wait in your singleness to someone else's time being single. Do not compare any season in your life to someone else's season. Period. God will uniquely work things out for you (Romans 8:28)! Trust His timing.

Continue to serve God and pursue your purpose while you wait. Your season of singleness may be a few months, one year, or a couple of years. No matter how long you wait, pass the test, and wait well! Be a good servant to God on your job, in your community, to your children, in school, and in all that you do (Colossians 3:23-24). Consume yourself with work and stay busy in the Lord. Stay focused on Him, what He has called you to do, and continue to be still. At the right time, you will cross paths with a man of God, and your singleness will come to an end. Write down your standards and expectations. Review them daily, and do not settle! Wait for the man that you believe is God's best for your life. When it is time to move forward into a relationship, consult with God. He will help guide you into choosing the best partner for your life.

> "But they that wait upon the Lord shall renew their strength; they shall mount up on wings as eagles; they shall run, and not be weary; and they shall walk, and not faint."
> Isaiah 40:31 KJV

Affirmation

I will wait with love, hope, faith, and expectation, not frustration. In my waiting process, humble me. Help me to be patient and enduring. "Lord, I want your will in your timing not mine. I do not want to be ahead of you, nor do I want to be behind you. Help me, Father, to wait patiently on you!" (Joyce Meyer, Battlefield of the Mind).

HOW TO REST IN YOUR SEASON OF SINGLENESS

- Day 20 -
Forever Single

> "A woman who is no longer married or has never been married can be devoted to the Lord and holy in body and spirit. But a married woman has to think about her earthly responsibilities and how to please her husband. I am saying this for your benefit, not to place restrictions on you. I want you to do whatever will help you serve the Lord best, with few distractions as possible."
> 1 Corinthians 7:34-35 NLT

As you persist in waiting on God for your singleness to come to an end, continue to undividedly devote yourself to Him. Consume yourself with God! Keep your eyes on Him and engulf yourself in His love. Affirm His love over your life daily; believe and receive it! His love has the power to fill every void in your life. Walk in God's love, wear His love, and extend it to someone else today. Get lost in Him. Delight yourself in the Lord and in being alone. When marriage comes, there will be more responsibilities and new difficulties. Your marriage will be tested in unthinkable ways. So, fill your down time with God. He is still completing a work in you and making you whole.

Singleness is an opportunity to grow closer to Christ, build a solid foundation in your relationship with God, and achieve your individual goals. It is an opportunity for extreme personal and spiritual development. This is also the time to recognize/acknowledge your worth and create the standard for your future relationship. Your singleness is a gift from God. You have time to accomplish all you can with Him before you commit yourself to a life partner. You will gain so much in this season with God and in community with other believers. If you do not choose to be happy and content with being single, then you will not be happy and content in marriage. A relationship or marriage will not complete you. It will not satisfy your loneliness and unexpected discontentment. A relationship with Christ will! When you die, you cannot take your earthly relationships, jobs, and accomplishments with you. This world [everything in, of, and attached to it] is not your home. Your treasure and home is in heaven, and your everlasting promise is Jesus! In Him, you will find everything· healing, deliverance, deep satisfaction, love and pure joy.

Naked and alone you came into this world from your mother's womb, therefore; naked you will leave (Job 1·21)! Jesus Christ is coming back for you; you are His precious bride! Cleanse and prepare yourself daily for His return. He wants to marry you and become one with you in spirit and in truth. Marry Christ. He is everything you need and more. I encourage you to become content in your relationship with Him, and daily say "Yes," to the Man above!

In Revelation, there is a prophecy of events of what was, what is, and what will come on Earth before the second coming of the Lord. The prophecy describes heavenly worship. In heaven, we will worship our Lord Jesus Christ for eternity. In heaven you will be single forever. You will be devoted to and in companionship with Jesus for eternity.

The time is now to express true worship to your Creator and King in a way that is genuine from your heart. Our Father is looking for those who will solely worship Him more than His blessings. Quit idolizing marriage, relationships, and the promises of God, for these things are temporary. Your relationship with Christ is eternal. It will last forever. Do not hold onto your life so tightly. Instead, when things get tough in your singleness, cling to God and His Word (Matthew 10:39).

Remember, God will do what He said He would do. He is a true Man of His Word. The more you obey and surrender to Him, He will begin fulfilling the promises He made to you. Until then, find rest in His loving arms, and relax in His presence. Stay committed to being intentional in your devotion to God in your season of singleness. As you devote yourself to Him, He will cover you in this season. When difficulties arise in other seasons of life, do not be shaken. Be steadfast and rooted in Christ. Stand firm and believe God will always have everything under control in your life. Forever trust Him and be still.

"For everything there is a season, a time for every activity under heaven...Yet God has made everything beautiful for its own time. He has planted eternity in the human heart, but even so, people cannot see the whole scope of God's work from beginning to end. So, I conclude there is nothing better than to be happy and enjoy ourselves as long as we can."
Ecclesiastes 3: 1 & 11-12 NLT

Encouraging songs to listen to that will carry you through singlehood as you rest in it.

1. "Be Still"- Travis Greene
2. "Good Good Father"- Chris Tomlin
3. "Never Leave"- Isaac Robinson
4. "I Shall Not Want"- Audrey Assad
5. "The Way That You Love Me"- Johnathan McReynolds
6. "PEACE"- Hillsong Young & Free
7. "Potter"- Tamela Mann
8. "Still"- Mali Music
9. "Solid Rock"- Tasha Cobbs Leonard
10. "Gracefully Broken"- Tasha Cobbs Leonard
11. "Maranatha"- Jackie Hill-Perry
12. You Keep on Getting Better"- Maverick City Music

About the Author

Ariel Green is a leader, writer, dance worshiper, and prophetic dancer. She is passionate about encouraging others and leading women to Christ. Ariel has a bachelor's degree in Social Work and is a social worker in her community. Ariel's mission is to teach others how to overcome childhood traumas, end generational curses, and prosper in life with Christ. She resides in Baton Rouge, Louisiana.

HOW TO REST IN YOUR SEASON OF SINGLENESS

www.ingramcontent.com/pod-product-compliance
Lightning Source LLC
Chambersburg PA
CBHW030311100526
44590CB00012B/587